G000298765

Cottage Flowers

The tiniest garden is often the loveliest. Look at our cottage gardens, if you need to be convinced.

Vita Sackville-West

Cottage Flowers

Marie Angel

Pelham Books

Acknowledgements

I am grateful to the following for permission to include copyright material in this anthology:
Batsford Ltd for *The English Cottage* by Harry Batsford and Charles Fry; Mrs Nicolete Gray and
The Society of Authors on behalf of the Laurence Binyon Estate for *The Burning of the Leaves* by
Laurence Binyon; William Heinemann Ltd for *Early to Rise* by Bob Copper;
Routledge & Kegan Paul Ltd for *Gardener's Choice* by E. Dunbar and C. Mahoney;
BBC Publications Ltd for *A Child of the Forest* by Winifred Foley; Longman Group Ltd for *Old West
Surrey* and *Wood and Garden* by Gertrude Jekyll; Batsford Ltd for *Surrey Gardens* by Eric Parker;
The Medici Society Ltd for *The Story of the Garden* by Eleanor Sinclair Rohde; Curtis Brown Ltd for
In Your Garden, In Your Garden Again, More for Your Garden, Even More for Your Garden by
Vita Sackville-West; David Higham Associates Ltd for *Down to Earth* by Anne Scott James and published
by Michael Joseph Ltd; The Executors of the Estate of Miss Ermengard Maitland for *Hoops at Dusk*
by Fredegond Shove; Oxford University Press for *Lark Rise to Candleford* by Flora Thompson;
Faber and Faber Ltd for *Country Hoard* by Alison Uttley; Secker & Warburg Ltd for *Autumn Seeds*
from Andrew Young's *Complete Poems*, edited by Leonard Clark.

   Finally, my thanks are due to my sister and all my friends who so willingly robbed their gardens to
keep me supplied with specimens; to the staff at Caterham Valley Library for their help in finding the
books I needed; to the Berkshire Central Library for sending me details of Mary Russell Mitford's
cottage; and lastly, to Muriel Gascoin, who not only gave me the idea and encouraged me throughout,
but shouldered a great deal of the work as well.

First published by
Pelham Books Ltd
44 Bedford Square
London WC1B 3DU
1980

ISBN 0 7207 1259 9

Printed and bound in Italy by Arnoldo Mondadori, Verona

Contents

Introduction	7
Aconites/Snowdrops/Ivy	9
Lent Lily (Wild Daffodil)/Periwinkle/Crocus	10
White Violets/Primrose/Wallflowers	11
Cowslips	12
Polyanthus/Lenten Roses (Hellebores)	13
Bachelor's Buttons/Tulip/Lily of the Valley	14
Double Primrose	15
Musk Rose/Common Jasmine/White Zonal Pelargonium/ Honeysuckle	16
Nasturtiums/Pot Marigold (*Calendula*)	17
Show Auriculas	19
Rabbit's Ears (*Stachys lanata*)/Violas	20
Viola—Irish Mollie	21
Old Roses—including Rosa Mundi, Boule de Neige, Charles de Mills	23
Lobelia/Rose—Little White Pet/Campion (*Viscaria*)/ Catmint (*Nepeta*)/Yarrow/Pink	24
Regal Pelargoniums/Zonal Pelargoniums	25
Pansy	26
Lobelia/Pot Marigold (*Calendula*)/French Marigolds/ Cornflowers	27
Old English Lavender/Snapdragon/Perennial Pea	28
Pinks	29
Fuchsias—including F. magellanica, F. fulgens, F. 'Coachman', F. 'Snowcap'	30
Sweetpea	32
Bellflower (*Campanula*)/Pansy/Crane's Bill (Geranium)/ Borage	33

Strawberry plant   34
Dutch Iris/Laced Pinks/Snapdragon/Candytuft/Purple Sage 35
Pansies   36
Hollyhocks   37
Dahlias—Bishop of Llandaff/Sunflower   39
Japanese Anemones/Ivy-leaved Toadflax   40
Sowbread (*Cyclamen neapolitanum*)   41
Michaelmas Daisies/Chrysanthemums/Bramble   42
Phlox/Rue/Crane's Bill (Geranium)   43
Rosehips—Rosa rugosa   44
Cotoneaster/Winter Jasmine   47
Hazelnuts and catkins   48

Introduction

Cottage gardens date from the late Middle Ages, when flowering plants, in so far as they had a place at all among the onions and cabbages, were grown not for their beauty but for their usefulness : as simple medicines, as garnishes and flavourings, for wine-making, and to provide the cottager's bees with pollen and nectar. The flowers of the violet, for instance, were used in salads, as were those of the pot marigold ; and the early pinks were known as 'sops-in-wine' from the custom of dropping the flower heads into a glass of wine to flavour it.

Most of these early flowers—violets, cowslips, honeysuckle, dog roses—were brought in from the wild. Later, cultivated flowers drifted from the larger garden of the lord of the manor to the cottagers and were pushed into odd corners or used as borders to paths and vegetable plots. Some of these plants were quite exotic, for by Tudor and Elizabethan times flowers such as the jasmine from Persia and the tulip from Turkey had reached England.

By the seventeenth century flowers were sufficiently accepted for themselves in the cottage garden for some to be disparaged because of their popularity : as John Rea wrote in his *Flora* of the beautiful (and now rare) double primrose, 'were it not so common in every Countrywoman's garden, it would be more respected, for it is a sweet and dainty flower.'

Some of the flowers that we most closely associate today with cottage gardens—the auricula, polyanthus, and laced pink—were originally florists' flowers, that is flowers cultivated by specialist growers to an exacting perfection. They became cottage flowers partly because so many cottage craftsmen grew them in their gardens (and made a real contribution to developing certain famous strains, as for example the Paisley weavers and the Paisley pinks) and partly because, as fashions in flowers changed, some of these old flowers survived only in cottage gardens, having had to cede place to newer, larger and often showier flowers in the gardens of the wealthy.

The revival of interest in cottage gardens is due to the work of such writers —and gardeners—as William Robinson at the end of the nineteenth century, and more recently to Gertrude Jekyll, Vita Sackville-West and Marjorie Fish. Although their own gardens were on a much larger scale, they exploited the informality of the cottage garden and encouraged a new appreciation of the old flowers. Their influence is felt in all our gardens today.

[7]

The true cottage garden is now a very rare sight. But cottage gardening still has much to offer the modern gardener, for the very smallness of present-day plots has led to the rediscovery that it is perfectly possible to grow vegetables and flowers in a happy blend as the cottager did in the past. Perhaps, too, the old-fashioned flowers are coming back into favour as being more in scale with smaller gardens—a rejection of the overlarge forms so frequently offered by nurserymen today for the charm and sturdy character of the old favourites.

My own interest in cottages and their gardens began in the 1930s when I came to live in Warlingham. Later, my friendship with Charles and Dorothy Mahoney at the Royal College of Art led to visits to their sixteenth-century cottage in Kent. Charles had introduced many of the old flowers into his garden—peonies, hellebores, periwinkles (some from the garden of John Nash), auriculas, gold- and silver-laced polyanthus, old pinks, and above all the old shrub roses ; everything grew so exuberantly that one could hardly walk down the paths. Charles was often to be found sitting half-hidden among the thrusting foliage drawing his favourite sunflowers. He generously shared not only his knowledge of plants and how to draw them, but handed over many slips, seeds and roots to see if they would take in the flinty soil of my garden. Many did and still flourish today.

The flowers in this book were nearly all drawn directly from living specimens and as far as possible the habit of the plant is shown. Careful observation is necessary for a realistic representation, as every flower and every leaf is different from its fellow on the same stem. Drawing a plant from memory one never achieves this casual look which makes every plant individual.

In the list of Contents, the flowers are identified by their most usual common name, although many flowers have a different name in different parts of the country. *Stachys lanata*, for instance, is known variously as rabbit's ears, lamb's ears, lamb's tongue, lamb's lugs and Saviour's flannel, and *Antirrhinum* as snapdragons or bunny mouths. Occasionally, if it seems helpful, I've given the variety, but in the true tradition of cottage flowers some were unknown.

The quotations have been chosen to complement the flowers in the paintings. Some are contradictory ; some reflect a romantic view of the cottage garden ; others are a true and faithful record of country experience. But all will, I hope, evoke the beauty of the old flowers.

JANUARY   The lesser early bulbous Violet cometh into view, on a small Stalk about seven or eight Inches high, from between two pale green narrow Leaves, being a small pendulous Flower, with three pointed milk white Leaves on the out side, with three shorter, edged or tipt with green, fashioned like a Cup, their inside green, from a bulbous Root, round like that of a Daffadil ; a common Flower, yet not to be wanted, because when none other appears that does, though in the Snow, whence called Snow-Flower, or Snow-Drops, they increase by Roots, indeed too fast, ther fore their Pods are to be pull'd off when going to Seed : So hardy that they may be moved at any time.

from *The Florist's Vade-Mecum* (1683) by the Reverend Samuel Gilbert

. . . I am being strictly correct in comparing the varnished yellow of the winter aconite to our common buttercup, for they both belong to the same botanical order of the *Ranunculaceae*.

The proper name of the winter aconite is *Eranthis*. *Eranthis hyemalis* is the one usually grown, and its smudge of gold should be good enough for anybody. It has the great advantage of flourishing almost anywhere, in shade or sun, under trees or in the open, and also of producing a generous mustard- and-cress-like crop of self-sown seedlings which you can lift and transplant.

from *In Your Garden Again* by Vita Sackville-West

The women never worked in the vegetable
gardens or on the allotments, even when they had
their children off hand and had plenty of spare
time, for there was a strict division of labour
and that was 'men's work'. Victorian ideas, too,
had penetrated to some extent, and any work
outside the home was considered unwomanly.
But even that code permitted a woman to
cultivate a flower garden, and most of the houses
had at least a narrow border beside the pathway.
As no money could be spared for seeds or plants,
they had to depend upon roots and cuttings
given by their neighbours, and there was little
variety ; but they grew all the sweet old-fashioned
cottage garden flowers, pinks and sweet williams
and love-in-a-mist, wallflowers and forget-me-
nots in spring and hollyhocks and Michaelmas
daisies in autumn. Then there were lavender and
sweetbriar bushes, and southern-wood, sometimes
called 'lad's love', but known there as 'old man'.

from *Lark Rise* by Flora Thompson

Next to the Hyacinths appear the
Daffodils, some of which deserve
entertainment in your garden, to be
placed in your borders next your
Walls, or under Pales.

from *The Florist's Vade-Mecum* (1683) by the
Reverend Samuel Gilbert

March Violets of the Garden have a
great prerogative above others, not
only because the mind conceiveth a
certaine pleasure and recreation by
smelling and handling of those most
odoriferous Flowers, but also for that
very many by these Violets receive
ornament and comely grace : for
there bee made of them Garlands for
the head, Nosegaies and posies
which are delightfull to looke on and
pleasant to smell to, speaking
nothing of their appropriate vertues ;
yea Gardens·themselves receive by
these the greatest ornament of all,
chiefest beautie and most gallant
grace.

from *The Herball* (1597) by John Gerard

On one side is a gloomy garden, with
an old man digging in it, laid out in
straight dark beds of vegetables,
potatoes, cabbages, onions, beans ; all
earthy and mouldy as a newly dug
grave. Not a flower or flowering shrub !
Not a rose-tree or currant bush !
Nothing but for sober, melancholy use.
Oh, different from the long irregular
slips of the cottage-gardens, with their
gay bunches of polyanthuses and
crocuses, their wall-flowers sending
sweet odours through the narrow
casement, and their gooseberry-trees
bursting into a brilliancy of leaf, whose
vivid greenness has the effect of a
blossom on the eye !

from *Our Village* (1824) by Mary Russell Mitford

The neighbourhood of Manchester and
Macclesfield is justly celebrated for
producing the finest specimens of this
flower, and in these manufacturing
districts the criterion of a fine
polyanthus is ascertained with as
narrow a scrutiny as the sportsman
regards his pointer or setter dog !

from *Flora Historica* (1824) by H. Phillips

[12]

Few gardens lack the Polyanthus, for, apart from its beauty, it is such a generous grower, and divides so readily into any number of parts that everyone finds pleasure in giving pieces to everyone else. With the Primrose and the Auricula it comes in the early Spring, companioning the bulbs: Scillas and Narcissi, Grape Hyacinths and Fritillaries. Yet it has Summer-like qualities, its colour and scent and rich green leaves giving it a kind of warmth not possessed by the others.

from *Gardener's Choice* by E. Dunbar and C. Mahoney

[13]

On the border under the gooseberry
bushes were Bachelor's Buttons,
crimson and white round buttons to sew
on somebody's coat, and grey-green
Lad's Love, aromatic and delicious,
which the young women slyly inserted
in their bunches of flowers. There were
giant sunflowers, always turning their
broad country faces towards the sun
god, and little pansies, which my
mother called Love-in-idleness, in
many-coloured frocks, close together
like a class of children, eager to talk
and see all that was going on. There
were Snapdragons, with closed lips
ready to open and speak a silent word
if one pressed them, and lilies-of-the-
valley, with their ivory peals of bells
which surely rang when nobody was
about. They were the sisters of the
wild lilies in the woods.

from *Country Hoard* by Alison Uttley

There is something in all of us which responds to something we have known in our childhood. It may be a scent, or a touch, or a sight, or anything which evokes a memory. For some of us this evocation arises from the recollection of flowers we saw growing in our grandparents' gardens and now search for in vain.

Why should they have gone out of fashion, the dear old tenants of the kitchen garden border? They were not very grand, so they were usually relegated to the strip between the espalier apples and the path. They shared that strip with the old double primroses, and the Hen-and-Chicken daisy, and some Dusty Miller auriculas, all living very happily together. The plants I am thinking of now, came behind these lowly growers, into the middle-height of the border.

They all had English names by which we knew them. There was the Bleeding Heart or Lyre Flower, more familiar under that name than as *Dicentra* or *Dielytra spectabilis*. One could pull each locket of the Bleeding Heart into different shapes, the most pleasing turning into a little pink-and-white ballet dancer. If you don't believe me, try it. Then there was Masterwort, or *Astrantia*, a greenish-white or pale pink, a reliable old plant for the border, so seldom seen now. Then there was Solomon's Seal, *Polygonatum multiflorum*; and *Smilacina racemosa*, both plants for a shady place, with grand green leaves and long strands of white moonlight flowers. The Smilacina has the advantage of a strong scent and of lasting very well in water. It deserves to be grown much more extensively.

Another old plant I like very much is *Tradescantia virginiana*, the Spiderwort named after John Tradescant, gardener to Charles I and Henrietta Maria. It is also called the Trinity Flower, owing to its three petals of a rich violet, curiously lurking amongst the grassy leaves.

from *Even More for Your Garden* by Vita
Sackville-West

There is scarcely a cottage without some plants in the window; indeed, the windows are often so much filled up with them that the light is too much obscured. The wise cottagers place them outside in the summer, to make fresh growth and gain strength.

The old double white rose, brother of the pretty pink Maiden's Blush, never seems so happy or looks so well as in a cottage garden; and the old kinds of cluster roses are great favourites.

The deep-rooting Everlasting Pea (Winter-bean is its local name) is a fine old cottage plant, and Nasturtiums ramble far and wide. Nowhere else does one see such Wallflowers, Sweet-Williams, and Canterbury Bells, as in these carefully-tended little plots.

It is a sign of careful gardening and good upbringing, when the little boys of a family are seen on the roads with old shovels and little improvised hand-carts, collecting horse-droppings. It means that the plants will have a nourishing surface mulching, that will be much to their benefit.

from *Old West Surrey* by Gertrude Jekyll

In summer they sat in kitchen chairs on their doorsteps knitting or busy with needle and mending-thread. Through the polished panes of narrow casements draped with white lace curtains, cats could be seen curled up asleep beside the potted cyclamen or geranium which, in many cases, shared the window-sill with jam-jars full of pale, yellowish liquid in which small blobs of yeast culture surfaced and sank with monotonous regularity like restless balls of cotton-wool. This was 'bee-wine' in the making and so called because the fluffy pieces of yeast were known as 'Jerusalem bees'. They were 'fed' on sugar and after a week or two in a warm window, the water, with which the process had been started, was miraculously turned into wine and all for the price of a few spoonsful of sugar.

from *Early to Rise* by Bob Copper

See how the Bears ears in their several dresses,
(That yet no Poet's Pen too high expresses.)
Each Head adorned with such rich attire,
Which Fools and Clouns may slight, whilst skill'd admire.
Their Gold, their Purples, Scarlets, crimson dies
Their dark and lighter hair'd Diversities.
With all their pretty shades and Ornaments,
Their parti-colour'd Coats and pleasing Scents.
Gold laid on scarlet, silver on the blue
With sparkling eyes to take the eyes of you.
Mixt Colours, many more to please that sense,
Others with rich and great magnificence;
In double Ruffs, with Gold and Silver laced,
On purple crimson, and so neatly placed,
Ransack *Flora's* wardrobes, none sure can bring,
More taking Ornaments t'adorn the Spring.

The Auricula from *The Florist's Vade-Mecum* (1683)
by the Reverend Samuel Gilbert

My Auriculas are not as good as they should be in a
Lancashire garden, for of all flowers it is the old Lancashire
favourite. It is still known as the Basier (a corruption, no
doubt, of Bear's Ear), and a pretty Lancashire ballad ends
every verse with the refrain:

'For the Basiers are sweet in the morning of May.'

from *A Year in a Lancashire Garden* (1879) by Henry Bright

Oft I have brought thee flowers, on their stalks set
Like vestal primroses, but dark velvet
Edges them round, and they have golden pits.

from *Endymion* by John Keats

Not the smallest and dryest garden should be without *Stachys lanata*, a white woolly leaved plant, called Rabbit's Ears by cottage children, and particularly attractive to some people, who through life retain the love of a child for something woolly and soft. Certain characteristics are always reminding us, especially in some women, even when old, that they were once children.

from *Pot-pourri from a Surrey Garden* (1898) by Alice Morse Earle

[20]

Old Man, or Lad's-love,—in the name there's nothing
To one that knows not Lad's-love, or Old Man,
The hoar-green feathery herb, almost a tree,
Growing with rosemary and lavender.
Even to one who knows it well, the names
Half decorate, half perplex, the thing it is :
At least, what that is clings not to the names
In spite of time. And yet I like the names.
The herb itself I like not, but for certain
I love it, as some day the child will love it
Who plucks a feather from the door-side bush
Whenever she goes in or out of the house.
Often she waits there, snipping the tips and shrivelling
The shreds at last on to the path, perhaps
Thinking, perhaps of nothing, till she sniffs
Her fingers and runs off. The bush is still
But half as tall as she, though it is as old ;
So well she clips it. Not a word she says ;
And I can only wonder how much hereafter
She will remember, with that bitter scent,
Of garden rows, and ancient damson trees
Topping a hedge, a bent path to a door,
A low thick bush beside the door, and me
Forbidding her to pick.

from *Old Man* by Edward Thomas

One of the first gardens I wrote about was Mrs Fish's at East
Lambrook Manor, and not only was Mrs Fish the most generous of
gardeners, but her garden was so thickly planted that when she dug
up a plant for you, stray roots of surrounding plants came up with it,
and you got a sort of lucky dip. I used to nurture these bits and
pieces and they always grew. Some of these stray hairs grew into a
colony of pink astrantias and others into a clump of white species
phlox ; and there was the old-fashioned pansy, Irish Mollie, which
Mrs Fish called Dirty Mollie, because it has a brown-and-yellow face
in need of a wash.

from *Down to Earth* by Anne Scott James

One cold slate-coloured morning towards the end of March, I received a note from a Nottingham mechanic, inviting me to assist in a judicial capacity at an exhibition of Roses, given by working men, which was to be held on Easter Monday. Not having at the time a Rose in my possession, although, to my shame be it spoken, I had ample room and appliances, it never occurred to me that the tiny glass houses, which I had seen so often on the hills near Nottingham, could be more honourably utilised or worthily occupied, and I threw down the letter on my first impulse as a hoax, and a very poor one.

On Easter Monday, in due course, upon a raw and gusty day, I went to Nottingham. Nor were my silly suspicions expelled until my hansom from the station stopped before the General Cathcart Inn, and the landlord met me, with a smile on his face and with a Senateur Vaisse in his coat, which glowed amid the gloom like the red light on a midnight train, and (in my eyes, at any rate) made summer of that damp and dismal day.

'The Roses were ready : would I go upstairs?' And upstairs, accordingly, with my co-censor, a nurseryman and skilled Rosarian of the neighbourhood, I mounted, and entered one of those long narrow rooms in which market-ordinaries are wont to be held.

I have never seen better specimens of cut Roses, grown under glass, than those which were exhibited by these working men. Their Tea-Roses—Adam, Devoniensis, Madame Willermorz, and Souvenir d'un Ami especially—were shown in their most exquisite beauty ; and, coming down to the present time, I do not hesitate to say that the best Maréchal Niel and the best Madame Margottin which I have yet seen, I saw this spring at Nottingham, in ginger-beer bottles ! Of course, in an exhibition of this kind, with difficulties to oppose which few dare to encounter and very few overcome, these poor florists must include among their masterpieces many specimens of medium merit, and some failures. Among the latter I cannot forget a small and sickly exposition of Paul Ricaut, who, by some happy coincidence, which warmed my whole body with laughter, was appropriately placed in a large medicine-bottle, with a label, requesting that the wretched invalid might be well rubbed every night and morning. Poor Paul ! a gentle touch would have sent him to *pot-pourri* !

When the prizes were awarded we left the show-room . . . I went with some of them to inspect their gardens. These are tiny allotments on sunny slopes, just out of the town of Nottingham, separated by hedges or boards, in size about three to the rood. And yet it was delightful to see how much might be, and was, done in one of these pleasant plots. There was something for every season : There, to cheer the ungenial days of winter, were the Christmas Rose, the Aconite, the Laurestinus, the Golden Holly, the Cheimonanthus fragrans on its snug bit of southern wall, with the large yellow Jasmine near, and the winter Violets beneath. There, to follow in the spring, the Mezereon, the Erica, the Berberis, the Snowdrop, Hepatica, Polyanthus, Crocus, and Tulip ; after these the Lilac, Laburnum, Ribes, and then the Royal Rose.

abridged from *A Book about Roses* (1869) by Dean Hole

The garden was a large one, tailing off at the bottom into a little field where Dick grew his corn crop. Nearer the cottage were fruit trees, then the yew hedge, close and solid as a wall, which sheltered the beehives and enclosed the flower garden. Sally had such flowers, and so many of them, and nearly all of them sweet-scented! Wallflowers and tulips, lavender and sweet william, and pinks and old-world roses with enchanting names—Seven Sisters, Maiden's Blush, moss rose, monthly rose, cabbage rose, blood rose, and, most thrilling of all to the children, a big bush of the York and Lancaster rose, in the blooms of which the rival roses mingled in a pied white and red. It seemed as though all the roses in Lark Rise had gathered together in that one garden. Most of the gardens had only one poor starveling bush or none; but, then, nobody else had so much of anything as Sally.

from *Lark Rise* by Flora Thompson

Nostalgia for the past has brought with it
a revival of taste for the old-fashioned
flowers : the flaked pinks and carnations,
the double primroses, the old roses, the
broken tulips, the double Sweet William.
Perhaps it is not only nostalgia for an age
which, rightly or wrongly, we esteem
to have been happier than our own, as it
was certainly more leisurely, but also a
natural reaction against the exaggerated
blooms we are offered today : size not
subtlety.

from *In Your Garden Again* by Vita Sackville-West

Cottage people and people living in rural
villages always seem so clever and so
green-fingered about this sort of thing.
They keep plants on their window-sills,
flourishing for years, without any light or
any attention at all, or so it seems. We
might all usefully take a tip from the
cottagers, and grow more pot-plants to
set out of doors during the summer
months and to bring indoors as soon as
frost threatens, and then just to set them
down on a window-sill in a room warmed
by an ordinary fire, enough to keep the
frost out.

from *More for Your Garden* by Vita Sackville-West

Next to her poultry our good farmer's wife loved her flower garden; and, indeed, it was of the very first water, the only thing about the place that was fine. She was a real, genuine florist; valued pinks, tulips, and auriculas, for certain qualities of shape and colour, with which beauty has nothing to do; preferred black ranunculuses, and gave in to all those obliquities of a triple-refined taste by which the professed florist contrives to keep pace with the vagaries of the Bibliomaniac. Of all odd fashions, that of dark, gloomy, dingy flowers, appears to me the oddest. Your true *connoisseurs* now shall prefer a deep puce hollyhock to the gay pink blossoms which cluster round that splendid plant like a pyramid of roses. So did she. The nomenclature of her garden was more distressing still. One is never thoroughly sociable with flowers till they are naturalised, as it were, christened, provided with decent, homely, well-wearing English names. Now her plants had all sorts of heathenish appellations, which—no offence to her learning —always sounded wrong. I liked the bees' garden best; the plot of ground immediately round their hives, filled with common flowers for their use, and literally 'redolent of sweets'. Bees are insects of great taste in every way, and seem often to select for beauty as much as for flavour. They have a better eye for colour than the florist. The butterfly is also a *dilettante*. Rover though he be, he generally prefers the blossoms that become him best. What a pretty picture it is, in a sunshiny autumn day, to see a bright spotted butterfly, made up of gold and purple and splendid brown, swinging on the rich flower of the china-aster!

from *Our Village* (1824) by Mary Russell Mitford

[26]

. . . There was no such thing known then as planting potatoes
in the field, and this made every foot of the garden ground
so precious that people could not spare room for flower beds.
Some of the old women would have a flower border and
raise a few pinks and roses and a little thyme and lad's love,
make up the flowers into knots and nosegays, and sell them
at a halfpenny apiece. The lads would buy them and stick
them in their hats on Sundays. Nosegays were very much
sought after.

from the Reverend Francis Kilvert's *Diary*

The pinks along my garden walks
Have all shot forth their summer stalks,
Thronging their buds 'mong tulips hot,
And blue for-get-me-not.

Their dazzling snows forth-bursting soon
Will lade the idle breath of June :
And waken thro' the fragrant night
To steal the pale moonlight.

The nightingale at end of May
Lingers each year for their display,
Till when he sees their blossoms blown,
He knows the spring is flown.

June's birth, they greet, and when their bloom
Dislustres, withering on his tomb,
Then summer hath a shortening day ;
And steps slow to decay.

Pinks by Robert Bridges

Little strips in front of roadside cottages have a
simple and tender charm that one may look for
in vain in gardens of greater pretension. And
the old garden flowers seem to know that there
they are seen at their best; for where else can one
see such Wall-flowers, or Double Daisies, or
White Rose bushes; such clustering masses of
perennial Peas, or such well-kept flowery
edgings of Pink, or Thrift, or London Pride?

from *Wood and Garden* by Gertrude Jekyll

Mrs Master's fuchsias hung
Higher and broader, and brightly swung,
    Bell-like, more and more
Over the narrow garden-path,
Giving the passer a sprinkle-bath
       In the morning.

She put up with their pushful ways,
And made us tenderly lift their sprays,
    Going to her door :
But when her funeral had to pass
They cut back all the flowery mass
       In the morning.

The Lodging House Fuchsias by Thomas Hardy

Four introductions of the late eighteenth and early nineteenth centuries captured the cottager's fancy—the American currant, the fuchsia, the scarlet geranium and musk. One of the earliest fuchsias to flower in England was a plant on a cottage window-sill. James Lee, the great nurseryman of the late eighteenth century, saw a pot of it in flower in a small house in Wapping. The woman refused at first to listen to his offers to buy it, for it had been brought her by her husband, who was a sailor. Ultimately she reluctantly parted with it for eight guineas coupled with the promise of two of the first plants raised from it.

from *The Story of the Garden* by Eleanour Sinclair Rohde

James Lee was the true plantsman, always prepared to hand on information about the latest novelties, a complete contrast to Philip Miller, curator of the Chelsea Physic Garden, who preferred to conceal the names and origin of his greatest treasures. This contributed in no small degree to Lee's reputation. Evidently all the wrappings of the foreign seeds that arrived at Chelsea were dropped into the Thames, and Lee is said to have kept a boy for the express purpose of retrieving them, even if he had to swim.

With Mr. Lee's discovery the gardening public took the Fuchsia to its heart, and for more than a century its graceful blooms had a vogue such as few garden flowers have ever enjoyed. Fashions in flowers change just as they do in clothes, houses, and gardens, and so the Fuchsia suffered an eclipse when public taste veered round to ribbon borders and carpet beds, and the great influx of hardy annuals that reached Europe towards the end of last century. Many of the favourites of eighty years ago are forgotten, and it is only in the pages of old gardening periodicals that we find some memory of their charm and beauty.

Of the fifteen hundred or so named varieties known in those days, scarcely one-third survive, and this has brought home to us that something precious has been lost with so many of those old-world favourites. The desire to revive an interest in them is world-wide and has led to the formation of the American and British Fuchsia Societies, which have already been responsible for bringing back some of the old varieties from the window ledges, cemeteries, and old-fashioned gardens where they sought sanctuary in days gone by.

from *The Coming of the Flowers* by A. W. Anderson

In nearly all the cottages there was but one room downstairs, and many of these were poor and bare, with only a table and a few chairs and stools for furniture and a superannuated potato-sack thrown down by way of hearthrug. Other rooms were bright and cosy, with dressers of crockery, cushioned chairs, pictures on the walls and brightly coloured hand-made rag rugs on the floor. In these there would be pots of geraniums, fuchsias, and old fashioned sweet-smelling musk on the window-sills.

from *Lark Rise* by Flora Thompson

Here are sweetpeas, on tip-toe for a flight:
With wings of gentle flush o'er delicate white,
And taper fingers catching at all things,
To bind them all about with tiny rings.

from '*I stood tip-toe upon a little hill*' by John Keats

'Wey!' cried Charlie to the leading team, as they drew level with the cottages where we stood waiting, and with a rattle of trace-chains and an impatient flinging about of heads the horses pulled to a halt. Standing on the shafts, he took me from mother and chucked me up on top of the load as high as the cottage eaves and I found myself bouncing on the huge mattress of bales and looking in through the attic window from which, standing in my night shirt, I had so lately been looking out. Dad's pigeons, a mixed bunch of tumblers, blue-rocks and fan-tails, strutted tenderly about on pink feet skidding on the sloping tiles and rummaging in the creeper and rambler roses which were draped over the dormer window like a shawl.

 . . . Two hundred yards along the road we stopped to pick up cousin Ron and, being that much older than I, he grabbed one of the ropes by which the bales were securely lashed down and shinned up it like a shell-back. Then off we went at a steady four miles an hour down the familiar road, past New Barn where the mellow tiles of the roof, ranging in colour from brick-red to mauve and stained in places with the yellow and orange of lichen, shone in the morning like Joseph's coat.

from *Early to Rise: a Sussex Boyhood* by Bob Copper

[32]

We have a cat, a magnificent animal, so large and powerful that, if he were in the army, he would be called Long Tom. He is a cat of fine disposition, the most irreproachable morals I ever saw thrown away in a cat, and a splendid hunter . . . The companionship of Calvin, also, counts for a good deal. He usually attends me, unless I work too long in one place; sitting down on the turf, displaying the ermine of his breast, and watching my movements with great intelligence. He has a feline and genuine love for the beauties of Nature, and will establish himself where there is a good view, and look on it for hours . . .

I wish I knew as much about natural history and the habits of animals as Calvin does. He is the closest observer I ever saw; and there are few species of animals on the place that he has not analyzed. I think that he has, to use a euphemism very applicable to him, got outside of every one of them, except the toad. To the toad he is entirely indifferent; but I presume he knows that the toad is the most useful animal in the garden.

from *My Summer in a Garden* (1898) by Charles Dudley Warner

To the broad coping stone of the wall under the lime-boughs speckled thrushes came almost hourly to peer out and reconnoitre if it was safe to visit the garden, sometimes to see if a snail had climbed up the ivy. They then dropped quietly down into the long strawberry patch immediately under. The cover of strawberries is the constant recourse of all creeping things; the thrushes looked round every plant and under every leaf and runner. One toad always resided there, often two, and as you gathered a ripe strawberry you might catch sight of his black eye watching you take the fruit he had saved for you.

Richard Jeffries

And now when sheering of the flocks are done
Some ancient customs mixd wi harmless fun
Crowns the swains merry toils—the timid maid
Pleasd to be praisd and yet of praise affraid
Seeks her best flowers not those of woods and fields
But such as every farmers garden yield
Fine cabbage roses painted like her face
And shining pansys trimmd in golden lace
And tall tuft larkheels feathered thick wi flowers
And woodbines climbing oer the door in bowers
And London tufts of many a mottld hue
And pale pink pea and monkshood darkly blue
And white and purple jiliflowers that stay
Lingering in blossom summer half away
And single bloodwalls of a lucious smell
Old fashiond flowers which huswives love so well
And columbines stone blue or deep night brown
Their honey-comb-like blossoms hanging down
Each cottage gardens fond adopted child
Tho heaths still claim them where they yet grow wild
Mong their old companions summer blooms
Furze brake and mozzling ling and golden broom
Snap dragons gaping like to sleeping clowns
And 'clipping pinks' (which maidens sunday gowns
Full often wear catcht at by tozing chaps)
Pink as the ribbons round their snowy caps
'Bess in her bravery' too of glowing dyes
As deep as sunsets crimson pillowd skyes
And marjoram notts sweet briar and ribbon grass
And lavender the choice of every lass
And sprigs of lads love all familiar names
Which every garden thro the village claims

from *The Shepherd's Calendar* by John Clare

[36]

Divided from the shop by a narrow yard, and opposite the shoemaker's,
is a habitation of whose inmates I shall say nothing. A cottage—no—
a miniature house, with many additions, little odds and ends of places,
pantries, and what not; all angles, and of a charming in-and-outness;
a little bricked court before one half, and a little flower-yard before
the other; the walls, old and weather-stained, covered with hollyhocks,
roses, honeysuckles, and a great apricot-tree; the casement full of
geraniums; (ah, there is our superb white cat peeping out from among
them) the closets (our landlord has the assurance to call them rooms)
full of contrivances and corner-cupboards; and the little garden
behind full of common flowers, tulips, pinks, larkspurs, peonies, stocks,
and carnations, with an arbour of privet, not unlike a sentry-box,
where one lives in a delicious green light, and looks out on the gayest
of all gay flower-beds. That house was built on purpose to show in
what exceedingly small compass comfort may be packed. Well, I will
loiter there no longer.

from *Our Village* (1824) by Mary Russell Mitford

We did not have to go many yards down the road before we took the little path leading to Grancher's garden gate. A steep bank sloped from the main road to the back of the cottage, which stood, snug from the worst of the winds, on a narrow plateau. It was fronted by a garden terraced with little dry-stone walls to stop it slipping down altogether into the sharp incline below.

The level ground extended to the gate, and to a bit of garden to the left of it. Here Grancher was busy, to our surprise, among a patch of flowers. We expected no enthusiastic welcome from Grancher, and were certainly not prepared to be beckoned over, and asked to tell : 'What d'ye think o' they, then?'

We had no words to express what we 'thought o' they'. 'They' were about twenty different species of dahlias, and each seemed incomparably beautiful until you looked at the next. Grancher's rough hands, embedded with pit dirt scars, knotty and gnarled with work, made a perfect foil for their loveliness as he cupped each bloom to show them to us.

Which was the best, the modest pale salmon one, blushing pinkly at her petal tips, or that purple majesty, the size of a tea-plate? Soft yellows, mauves and pinks, brilliant reds, proud as a rich sultan in his harem, Grancher showed off his beauties ; and his hands trembled with the ecstasy of it all.

'Oh, Grancher! They be the best flowers I've ever seen!' And so they seemed.

from *A Child in the Forest* by Winifred Foley

My sensations are all glossy, spruce, voluptuous, and fine : they wear a candied coat, and are in holiday trim. I see the beds of larkspur with purple eyes ; tall holy-oaks, red and yellow ; the broad sun-flowers, caked in gold, with bees buzzing round them ; wildernesses of pinks, and hot-glowing pionies ; poppies run to seed ; the sugared lily, and faint mignonette, all ranged in order, and as thick as they can grow.

from *Why Distant Objects Please* by William Hazlitt

Here, first, on the left of the dip, stand cottages with the hill rising sharply at their back ; so sharply, indeed, that the gardens of the first two of them are scaled by flights of stone steps rising from ground-level to the height of the cottage roof. Truly a steep task for gardeners, but hillside flower-lovers are not disturbed by height, and the steps slant upwards side by side with asters, marigolds, chrysanthemums, Michaelmas daisies and wall-flowers waiting for the spring. Bargate stone is what Surrey provides for Busbridge stair builders and roadside walls, and here at the top of the hill Nature has planted what I like to think may have been Tennyson's 'flower in the crannied wall', the little ivy-leaved toadflax. Downhill, with elms towering left and right above the valley of the road, cottages stand on either side ; here a bunch of cotoneaster next to a window where I remember catching sight of a fox-terrier puppy peering out between pots of pink geraniums, and close by orchard trees, apple and damson, high behind the bargate wall that rises from the road. Here again, we look from lavender and snapdragon on our left to white Japanese anemones opposite, and behind the anemones golden rod, chrysanthemums and Michaelmas daisies, backed by a high bank of St. John's wort.

from *Surrey Gardens* by Eric Parker

A cottage friend of mine who grows some superb cyclamen on her kitchen window-sill tells me that her grandmother advised her to water them with weak tea. This may sound like an old wife's tale, but the tales of some old wives sometimes turn out to be right.

There are two kinds of cyclamen: the Persian, which is the one your friends give you, and which is not hardy, and the small, out-door one, a tiny edition of the big Persian, as hardy as a snowdrop. These little cyclamen are among the longest-lived of garden plants. A cyclamen corm will keep itself going for more years than its owner is likely to live. They have other advantages: (1) they will grow under trees, for they tolerate, and indeed enjoy, shade; (2) they do not object to a limy soil; (3) they will seed themselves and (4) they will take you round the calendar by a judicious planting of different sorts. *C. neapolitanum*, for instance, will precede its ivy-like leaves by its little pink flower in late autumn, white flowers if you get the variety *album*; *C. coum*, pink, white, or lilac, will flower from December to March; *C. ibericum* from February to the end of March; *C. balearicum* will then carry on, followed by *C. repandum*, which takes you into the summer; and, finally, *C. europaeum* for the late summer and early autumn. Some botanists believe this to be a native; it was certainly recorded here in the reign of Queen Elizabeth, when, if beaten into little flat cakes, it was considered 'a good amorous medicine to make one in love'.

from *In Your Garden* by Vita Sackville-West

The west is changing, green succeeds on gold,
White stars begin to mount the bitter air,
      Slow dusk is coming on,
      Its velvet petals close
About the dying gardens and the roofs
Of sleepy cottages, with ivied eaves.

      These dahlias feel the dusk,
      Michaelmas daisies blue,
And marigolds hang down their coronals,
Rich with the last rays of the dying sun
      That has withdrawn its soul
      From the world's hollow cup—
Leaving this upland village to the care
Of candles and of fragrant autumn winds.

from *Hoops at Dusk* by Fredegond Shove

Scarcely ever are the kitchen-gardens
without their flower fringes, but it is in the
front space that the family can really let
itself go. The porch and walls are covered
with climbing roses, and the path to the
front door is flanked by beds edged with
dwarf box, which enclose a crowd of bright
blooms from May to September—
snowdrops, daffodils, primulas, columbines,
bluebells, lupins, followed by larkspurs,
lilies, snapdragons, pinks, sweet-williams,
stocks, asters and many more, with dahlias,
Michaelmas daisies, chrysanthemums to
finish off the season. Rows of hollyhocks
skirt the boundary hedge, and in one corner
a great old yew overshadows the cottage
well; its dark foliage makes an effective foil
to the bright flower-colours. Tennyson has
pleasantly summarised the variety of cottage
flower-plots :—

One looked all rose tree, and another wore
A close-set robe of jasmine sown with stars ;
This had a rosy sea of gillyflowers
About it ; this a milky way on earth,
Like visions in the Northern Dreamer's heavens,
A lily avenue climbing to the doors ;
One, almost to the martin-haunted eaves,
A summer burial deep in hollyhocks ;
Each its own charm . . .

from *The English Cottage* by Harry Batsford and Charles Fry

[43]

Today I think
Only with scents,—scents dead leaves yield,
And bracken, and wild carrot's seed,
And the square mustard field ;

Odours that rise
When the spade wounds the root of a tree,
Rose, currant, raspberry, or goutweed,
Rhubarb or celery ;

The smoke's smell, too,
Flowing from where a bonfire burns
The dead, the waste, the dangerous,
And all to sweetness turns.

It is enough
To smell, to crumble the dark earth,
While the robin sings over again
Sad songs of Autumn mirth.

Digging by Edward Thomas

Waxlights, though we are accustomed to overlook the fact, and rank them with ordinary commonplaces, are true fairy-tapers,—a white metamorphosis from the flowers, crowned with the most intangible of all visible mysteries—fire.

Then there is honey, which a Greek poet would have called the sister of wax,—a thing as beautiful to eat as the other is to look upon ; and beautiful to look upon too. What two extraordinary substances to be made by little winged creatures out of roses and lilies ! What a singular and lovely energy in Nature to impel those little creatures thus to fetch out the sweet and elegant properties of the coloured fragrances of the gardens, and to serve them up to us for food and light ! Honey to eat and waxen tapers to eat it by.

Leigh Hunt

Now is the time for the burning of the leaves.
They go to the fire; the nostril pricks with smoke
Wandering slowly into a weeping mist.
Brittle and blotched, ragged and rotten sheaves!
A flame seizes the smouldering ruin and bites
On stubborn stalks that crackle as they resist.

The last hollyhock's fallen tower is dust;
All the spices of June are a bitter reek,
All the extravagant riches spent and mean.
All burns! The reddest rose is a ghost;
Sparks whirl up, to expire in the mist: the wild
Fingers of fire are making corruption clean.

Now is the time for stripping the spirit bare,
Time for the burning of days ended and done,
Idle solace of things that have gone before:
Rootless hope and fruitless desire are there;
Let them go to the fire, with never a look behind.
The world that was ours is a world that is ours no more.

They will come again, the leaf and the flower, to arise
From squalor of rottenness into the old splendour,
And magical scents to a wondering memory bring;
The same glory, to shine upon different eyes.
Earth cares for her own ruins, naught for ours.
Nothing is certain, only the certain spring.

from *The Burning of the Leaves* by Laurence Binyon

[46]

Although a thoughtful bee still travels
And midge-ball ravels and unravels,
Yet strewn along the pathway lie
Like small open sarcophagi
The hazel-nuts broken in two
And cobwebs catch the seed-pearl dew.

Now summer's flowers are winter's weeds,
I think of all the sleeping seeds;
Winds were their robins and by night
Frosts glue their leafy cover tight;
Snow may shake down its dizzy feathers,
They will sleep safely through all weathers.

Autumn Seeds by Andrew Young